1

Unveiling the Mind

Nurturing Mental Health in a Chaotic World

Table of Contents

Disclaimer

This book provides a comprehensive exploration of mental health, its impact, and strategies for maintaining well-being in a fast-paced world while staying aligned with our life's purpose. Drawing on extensive research and observations of the human mind, the author incorporates insights from various sources to enhance our understanding and promote awareness of mental health. The words within the book serve as a valuable resource for learning and fostering a healthy mindset.

Introduction

In a fast-paced and demanding world, mental health has become a critical concern for individuals of all ages and backgrounds. "Unveiling the Mind" delves into the intricacies of mental health, offering a comprehensive guide to understanding, nurturing, and navigating the complexities of the human mind. Through a compassionate and empowering lens, this book aims to provide readers with the knowledge, tools, and support they need to foster positive mental well-being.

Negative mental health can have profound effects on individuals across the world. Here are a few practical examples illustrating the impact of negative mental health:

1. Depression: A person experiencing depression may exhibit symptoms such as persistent sadness, loss of interest in activities, changes in appetite or sleep patterns, and feelings of worthlessness. This can significantly impair their daily functioning, relationships, and overall quality of life.

2. Anxiety disorders: Individuals with anxiety disorders may constantly feel overwhelmed by excessive worry and fear. This can lead to avoidance of certain situations, panic attacks, and difficulties in social interactions, hindering their ability to pursue personal and professional goals.

3. Post-Traumatic Stress Disorder (PTSD): Someone who has experienced a traumatic event, such as war, natural disasters, or abuse, may develop PTSD. They may exhibit symptoms like flashbacks, nightmares, hypervigilance, and emotional distress. These symptoms can severely disrupt their ability to cope with daily life and form healthy relationships.

4. Substance abuse disorders: Negative mental health can contribute to the development of substance abuse disorders. Individuals may turn to drugs or alcohol as a way to self-medicate or numb emotional pain, leading to a cycle of addiction that further exacerbates their mental health struggles.

5. Eating disorders: Conditions such as anorexia nervosa, bulimia nervosa, or binge eating disorder can emerge as a result of negative mental health. These disorders can lead to severe physical and psychological consequences, including malnutrition, body image distortions, and social isolation.

6. Suicidal ideation: When mental health deteriorates significantly, individuals may experience thoughts of self-harm or suicide. This highlights the gravity of the impact negative mental health can have on a person's well-being and the importance of timely intervention and support.

These examples demonstrate the varied and far-reaching consequences of negative mental health on individuals worldwide. It emphasizes the need for increased awareness, destigmatization, and access to mental health resources and support.

The Landscape of Mental Health

The landscape of mental health refers to the overall state, understanding, and treatment of mental health conditions within a given society or community. It encompasses various factors such as prevalence rates of mental illnesses, awareness and education surrounding mental health, available resources and support systems, and approaches to diagnosis and treatment.

Understanding the landscape of mental health involves recognizing the diverse range of mental health conditions that individuals may experience, including anxiety disorders, mood disorders, psychotic disorders, personality disorders, and others. It also involves acknowledging the significant impact that mental health has on individuals' well-being, relationships, and overall quality of life.

In recent years, there has been an increasing recognition of the importance of mental health, leading to improved awareness and reduced stigma surrounding mental illness. Efforts have been made to promote mental health education, early intervention, and destigmatization, aiming to encourage individuals to seek help and support when needed.

Additionally, the landscape of mental health includes the availability and accessibility of mental health services. This includes the presence of mental health professionals such as psychiatrists, psychologists, therapists, and counselors, as well as the availability of appropriate treatment options, such as psychotherapy, medication, or a combination of both. Adequate funding, insurance coverage, and community support are essential factors in ensuring that mental health services are accessible to all individuals.

The landscape of mental health is dynamic and ever-evolving, influenced by societal attitudes, advancements in research and technology, and the recognition of the need for holistic approaches to mental well-being. Ongoing efforts are aimed at improving mental health literacy, reducing barriers to access, and promoting a comprehensive understanding of mental health that encompasses prevention, early intervention, and effective treatment.

Defining mental health and its significance in modern society

Mental health refers to a person's emotional, psychological, and social well-being. It encompasses how individuals think, feel, and behave, as well as their ability to handle stress, relate to others, and make choices. Mental health is of great significance in modern society because it affects every aspect of our lives.

Maintaining good mental health is essential for overall well-being and quality of life. It enables individuals to cope with the challenges and stresses of daily life, build and maintain positive relationships, and contribute productively to society. Mental health plays a crucial role in educational attainment, employment, and overall productivity.

In recent years, there has been a growing recognition of the importance of mental health in society. Increased awareness and understanding have helped reduce the stigma associated with mental health issues, encouraging more people to seek help and support. This has led to a greater focus on early intervention and prevention, promoting positive mental health practices, and providing accessible and effective treatment options.

Furthermore, mental health issues have significant economic implications. The World Health Organization estimates that mental health conditions cost the global economy over $1 trillion per year in lost productivity. By prioritizing mental health, societies can reduce these economic burdens and create more inclusive and resilient communities.

Overall, recognizing and addressing mental health needs is crucial for creating a healthier, happier, and more productive society. It requires collective efforts from individuals, communities, healthcare systems, and policymakers to ensure that mental health is given the attention, resources, and support it deserves.

Exploring the prevalence of mental health challenges globally

Exploring the prevalence of mental health challenges globally involves studying the frequency and distribution of various mental health conditions across different populations and regions worldwide. Researchers and experts gather data from surveys, studies, and existing literature to gain insights into the prevalence rates of disorders such as depression, anxiety, bipolar disorder, schizophrenia, and others.

By examining the prevalence of mental health challenges globally, we can better understand the magnitude of the issue and identify factors that contribute to the development of these conditions. This information helps policymakers, healthcare providers, and organizations develop targeted interventions, allocate resources effectively, and raise awareness about mental health on a global scale.

It's important to note that the prevalence of mental health challenges can vary significantly across countries and cultures due to factors like socio-economic conditions, access to healthcare, cultural attitudes towards mental health, and stigma. Therefore, comprehensive research and analysis are crucial to formulating effective strategies and promoting mental well-being worldwide.

Breaking down stigmas and misconceptions surrounding mental illness

Breaking down stigmas and misconceptions surrounding mental illness involves challenging and changing societal beliefs, attitudes, and perceptions about mental health conditions. Stigma refers to the negative attitudes, stereotypes, and discrimination that people with mental illnesses often face. These stigmas can lead to isolation, reluctance to seek help, and limited access to appropriate treatment and support.

To combat stigma, education and awareness play a vital role. Efforts should focus on providing accurate information about mental health, dispelling myths, and promoting understanding. This can be achieved through public campaigns, community programs, and school curricula that foster open discussions about mental health. Media outlets also play a crucial role in portraying mental health accurately and responsibly, avoiding sensationalism and reinforcing negative stereotypes.

Personal stories and experiences shared by individuals with mental health conditions and their loved ones can be powerful tools in challenging misconceptions. Such narratives help humanize mental illness, demonstrating that it can affect anyone and that recovery and successful management are possible with appropriate support.

Creating supportive and inclusive environments is equally important. Encouraging open conversations, fostering empathy, and promoting acceptance within families, workplaces, schools, and communities can help individuals feel safe and empowered to seek help when needed. Mental health services should be accessible, affordable, and integrated into primary healthcare systems to ensure that people receive timely and effective treatment without fear of judgment or discrimination.

By actively working to break down stigmas and misconceptions surrounding mental illness, we can create a more compassionate and inclusive society that supports the well-being and recovery of individuals living with mental health conditions.

Unraveling the Mind

"Unraveling the Mind" refers to the process of understanding and exploring the complexities of the human mind. It involves studying various aspects of cognition, perception, emotions, and behavior to gain insights into how the mind functions. Through scientific research, psychology, neuroscience, and related fields, researchers strive to unravel the intricate workings of the mind, including its underlying mechanisms, neural networks, and the interplay between biology and psychology. This pursuit of unraveling the mind can lead to a deeper understanding of human consciousness, mental processes, and ultimately contribute to advancements in various fields such as psychology, medicine, and artificial intelligence.

Understanding the inner workings of the human mind

Understanding the inner workings of the human mind involves studying the complex processes and mechanisms that govern human cognition, emotions, behavior, and perception. It encompasses various disciplines such as psychology, neuroscience, cognitive science, and philosophy.

Researchers aim to unravel how thoughts are formed, memories are stored and retrieved, decisions are made, and emotions are experienced. They investigate the neural networks and brain regions involved in different mental processes, utilizing techniques like neuroimaging, cognitive experiments, and computational modeling.

Additionally, understanding the human mind involves exploring conscious and unconscious mental processes, examining the influence of genetics and environment, and investigating the interplay between biological factors and psychological experiences.

By gaining insights into the inner workings of the human mind, researchers and professionals in fields like psychology and psychiatry can develop strategies to enhance mental well-being, treat psychological disorders, and improve cognitive performance. Moreover, this knowledge contributes to our understanding of human nature, self-awareness, and the fundamental questions of consciousness and identity.

Examining the interplay between biology, psychology, and environment

Examining the interplay between biology, psychology, and environment involves studying how these three factors interact and influence human behavior, cognition, and overall well-being.

Biology refers to the biological aspects of an individual, including genetic factors, brain structure and function, hormonal balance, and other physiological processes. These biological factors can influence various psychological aspects, such as personality traits, cognitive abilities, and susceptibility to certain mental health conditions.

Psychology focuses on the study of human thoughts, emotions, behaviors, and mental processes. It explores how individuals perceive and interpret the world, how they form beliefs and attitudes, and how they interact with others. Psychological factors can impact biological processes through mechanisms like stress responses, emotional regulation, and the placebo effect.

Environment encompasses the external surroundings and experiences that individuals encounter throughout their lives. This includes social interactions, cultural influences, family dynamics, socioeconomic factors, educational opportunities, and physical surroundings. The environment can shape and modify both biological and psychological factors, influencing an individual's development, attitudes, beliefs, and behaviors.

The interplay between biology, psychology, and environment is highly complex and dynamic. Biological factors can predispose individuals to certain psychological traits or vulnerabilities, while psychological factors can shape biological responses and adaptation. The environment can interact with both biology and psychology, either amplifying or mitigating their effects.

Studying this interplay is essential for understanding human behavior and mental health. It helps in identifying risk and protective factors, designing interventions and treatments, and promoting holistic approaches to well-being. Recognizing the intricate connections between biology, psychology, and environment provides a more comprehensive understanding of human nature and the factors that shape individual differences.

Uncovering the factors that contribute to mental health disorders

Understanding the factors that contribute to mental health disorders involves examining a range of influences on an individual's well-being. These factors can be multifaceted and interconnected, and they vary from person to person. Here are some key areas to consider when exploring the contributors to mental health disorders:

1. Biological Factors: Biological factors encompass genetic predispositions, neurochemical imbalances, and alterations in brain structure or function. Some mental health disorders have a hereditary component, suggesting that certain genes may increase vulnerability to specific conditions.

2. Psychological Factors: Psychological factors include an individual's cognitive and emotional processes, personality traits, coping mechanisms, and life experiences. Traumatic events, adverse childhood experiences, chronic stress, and low self-esteem can all impact mental health.

3. Environmental Factors: Environmental factors encompass the external circumstances and surroundings that individuals are exposed to. These may include socioeconomic status, family dynamics, cultural norms, access to healthcare, exposure to violence or trauma, and social support networks.

4. Social Factors: Social factors refer to interactions with others and the broader social environment. Social support, interpersonal relationships, discrimination, stigma, and social isolation can significantly influence mental health outcomes.

5. Lifestyle Factors: Lifestyle choices, such as diet, exercise, substance use, sleep patterns, and overall self-care practices, can impact mental well-being. Engaging in healthy behaviors can promote positive mental health, while unhealthy habits can increase vulnerability to mental health disorders.

It's important to note that mental health disorders often result from a complex interplay of these factors. Additionally, the exact combination and weight of these factors can vary widely among individuals. By understanding and addressing these contributing factors, mental health professionals can develop more comprehensive approaches to prevention, diagnosis, and treatment of mental health disorders.

Nurturing Emotional Resilience

Cultivating emotional intelligence and self-awareness

Cultivating emotional intelligence and self-awareness involves developing a deep understanding and awareness of one's own emotions, as well as the ability to recognize and empathize with the emotions of others. It is a process of enhancing emotional well-being and interpersonal relationships by honing these important skills.

Emotional intelligence encompasses several components, including self-awareness, self-regulation, motivation, empathy, and social skills. Self-awareness refers to recognizing and understanding one's own emotions, strengths, weaknesses, values, and motivations. It involves being attuned to one's emotional states, thoughts, and behavioral patterns.

By cultivating self-awareness, individuals can better understand how their emotions influence their thoughts and actions. This awareness enables them to make more conscious choices and respond to situations in a thoughtful and constructive manner. It also helps in identifying and managing one's own emotional triggers and biases.

Self-awareness is closely linked to emotional intelligence, as it forms the foundation for developing empathy and social skills. Empathy involves understanding and sharing the emotions of others, while social skills encompass effective communication, conflict resolution, and building positive relationships.

Cultivating emotional intelligence and self-awareness can have numerous benefits. It improves emotional resilience, allowing individuals to navigate challenging situations with greater ease. It enhances interpersonal relationships, as individuals become better attuned to the emotions and needs of others, fostering empathy and connection. It also promotes effective communication and collaboration, both in personal and professional settings.

Practices such as mindfulness meditation, journaling, seeking feedback from others, and engaging in self-reflection can help in developing emotional intelligence and self-awareness. These practices provide opportunities to observe and understand one's own emotions, thoughts, and behaviors, facilitating personal growth and enhanced emotional well-being.

Developing healthy coping mechanisms and stress management techniques

Developing healthy coping mechanisms and stress management techniques involves adopting strategies and practices to effectively handle and alleviate stress in a healthy and constructive manner. Here are some key points to understand:

1. Awareness: Recognize and acknowledge your stress triggers, emotions, and physical sensations associated with stress. Understand how stress affects you personally.

2. Self-Care: Prioritize self-care activities that promote physical, mental, and emotional well-being. This can include regular exercise, sufficient sleep, maintaining a balanced diet, and engaging in activities you enjoy.

3. Time Management: Efficiently manage your time and prioritize tasks. Break down larger tasks into smaller, manageable steps to avoid feeling overwhelmed. Set realistic goals and deadlines, and allocate time for relaxation and leisure.

4. Healthy Communication: Express your thoughts, feelings, and concerns to trusted individuals, such as friends, family, or a therapist. Effective communication can provide emotional support, different perspectives, and potential solutions.

5. Relaxation Techniques: Practice relaxation techniques like deep breathing exercises, meditation, mindfulness, or yoga. These techniques help calm the mind, reduce muscle tension, and promote overall relaxation.

6. Problem-Solving: Instead of dwelling on stressors, focus on finding solutions. Break down problems into smaller parts, brainstorm possible solutions, and take proactive steps to address them.

7. Positive Thinking: Cultivate a positive mindset by reframing negative thoughts. Challenge pessimistic or irrational thinking patterns and replace them with more realistic and positive perspectives.

8. Boundaries and Assertiveness: Set healthy boundaries to avoid overcommitting and feeling overwhelmed. Learn to say no when necessary and assert your needs in a respectful manner.

9. Social Support: Maintain a supportive network of friends, family, or support groups. Connecting with others can provide emotional support, outlets for sharing experiences, and a sense of belonging.

10. Hobbies and Relaxing Activities: Engage in activities that bring you joy and relaxation, such as hobbies, creative outlets, listening to music, reading, or spending time in nature.

Remember, developing healthy coping mechanisms and stress management techniques is an ongoing process. It requires self-reflection, practice, and patience to find what works best for you.

Fostering resilience in the face of adversity

Fostering resilience in the face of adversity refers to the process of developing and strengthening one's ability to bounce back and adapt in the midst of challenging or difficult circumstances. It involves cultivating the mental, emotional, and physical resources necessary to effectively cope with and overcome adversity.

Resilience is not an innate trait but rather a skill that can be nurtured and developed over time. Here are some key factors in fostering resilience:

1. Building a support network: Connecting with others who provide emotional support, encouragement, and practical assistance can help individuals navigate through adversity. Having a strong support system promotes resilience by offering a sense of belonging and reassurance during difficult times.

2. Developing coping strategies: Learning and practicing effective coping strategies helps individuals manage stress and adversity. Techniques such as problem-solving, positive reframing, mindfulness, and self-care can enhance resilience by promoting adaptability and emotional well-being.

3. Cultivating optimism and positive thinking: Adopting an optimistic mindset and focusing on positive aspects of a situation can contribute to resilience. Optimism enables individuals to maintain hope and view setbacks as temporary and manageable challenges, rather than insurmountable obstacles.

4. Enhancing self-belief and self-efficacy: Building confidence in one's abilities and strengths is essential for resilience. Recognizing past successes, setting achievable goals, and developing a belief in one's capacity to overcome adversity fosters resilience and empowers individuals to persevere in the face of challenges.

5. Embracing flexibility and adaptability: Resilient individuals are open to change and are willing to adapt their strategies and perspectives as needed. Flexibility allows for the exploration of new approaches and the ability to adjust to evolving circumstances, increasing the likelihood of successful outcomes.

6. Practicing self-care: Prioritizing self-care activities, such as maintaining a healthy lifestyle, getting enough rest, engaging in enjoyable hobbies, and seeking relaxation, supports resilience. Taking care of one's physical and mental well-being strengthens overall resilience and provides the energy and stamina needed to navigate challenging situations.

7. Learning from setbacks and failures: Resilient individuals view setbacks as opportunities for growth and learning. They reflect on past experiences, identify lessons learned, and apply them to future challenges. This mindset fosters resilience by promoting a proactive and adaptive approach to adversity.

Overall, fostering resilience in the face of adversity involves a combination of personal skills, supportive relationships, and positive mindset. By cultivating these factors, individuals can develop their ability to cope with adversity, adapt to change, and ultimately thrive in challenging circumstances.

Building a Supportive Network

Recognizing the importance of social connections and relationships
Recognizing the importance of social connections and relationships entails understanding the significance of human interaction and interpersonal bonds. It acknowledges that our connections with others play a vital role in our well-being and overall quality of life.

Social connections and relationships provide numerous benefits, both on an individual and collective level. They contribute to our emotional and mental health, providing support, empathy, and a sense of belonging. Strong relationships can enhance our resilience, reduce stress levels, and promote positive emotions.

Additionally, social connections have a profound impact on our physical health. Research indicates that individuals with strong social ties tend to have better cardiovascular health, stronger immune systems, and longer life expectancy. Having a network of supportive relationships can also help individuals navigate challenges, cope with adversity, and achieve personal growth.

Recognizing the importance of social connections and relationships encourages us to prioritize and nurture these bonds in our lives. It reminds us to invest time and effort in building and maintaining meaningful connections with family, friends, colleagues, and communities. By fostering these relationships, we create a supportive environment that enriches our lives and contributes to our overall well-being.

- Navigating interpersonal dynamics and conflict resolution:
Navigating interpersonal dynamics refers to the process of understanding and managing relationships and interactions between individuals. It involves recognizing and addressing the various factors that influence how people relate to one another, such as communication styles, personality differences, and power dynamics.

Conflict resolution, on the other hand, involves finding peaceful and mutually agreeable solutions to disagreements or conflicts that may arise in interpersonal relationships. It requires effective communication, active listening, empathy, and negotiation skills.

When navigating interpersonal dynamics and conflict resolution, it is important to promote open and honest communication, establish clear boundaries, and seek understanding and compromise. This often involves active listening to others' perspectives, expressing oneself assertively but respectfully, and finding common ground to reach resolutions that satisfy all parties involved.

Overall, navigating interpersonal dynamics and conflict resolution involves understanding, managing, and resolving conflicts or tensions in a constructive and respectful manner to foster healthy relationships and promote positive outcomes.

Seeking and providing support in times of need

Seeking and providing support in times of need refers to the act of reaching out for help or offering assistance when someone is going through a challenging or difficult period. It involves recognizing that individuals may require emotional, practical, or even financial support during such times and taking steps to address those needs.

When seeking support, individuals may reach out to friends, family members, or professional resources such as therapists or counselors. They may express their feelings, share their concerns, and ask for guidance or advice. By seeking support, individuals can gain different perspectives, receive emotional validation, and potentially find solutions to their problems.

On the other hand, providing support involves being there for someone who is in need. It can be as simple as lending a listening ear, offering empathy and understanding, or providing practical assistance. This support can come from family members, friends, or even community organizations. By offering support, individuals show care and compassion, creating a sense of connection and trust, which can greatly help those going through difficult times.

Both seeking and providing support in times of need are essential aspects of building and maintaining healthy relationships. They foster a sense of community, strengthen social bonds, and contribute to overall well-being. It's important to remember that everyone experiences challenges at some point in their lives, and by actively seeking or offering support, we can create a supportive and caring environment for ourselves and those around us.

Mindful Living and Self-Care

Embracing mindfulness practices for mental well-being

Embracing mindfulness practices can greatly benefit mental well-being. Mindfulness involves paying attention to the present moment with a non-judgmental and accepting attitude. By practicing mindfulness, individuals can develop a greater awareness of their thoughts, feelings, and sensations, which allows them to better understand and manage their mental states.

Engaging in mindfulness practices, such as meditation, deep breathing exercises, or body scans, can help reduce stress, anxiety, and depression. It encourages individuals to observe their thoughts and emotions without getting caught up in them, promoting a sense of detachment and inner peace.

Mindfulness also enhances self-awareness and self-compassion. By becoming more attuned to their internal experiences, individuals can recognize and acknowledge their emotions and needs, leading to a more compassionate and nurturing relationship with themselves.

Moreover, mindfulness can improve concentration and focus. By training the mind to stay present, individuals can enhance their ability to concentrate on tasks, make decisions, and respond effectively to challenges.

Overall, embracing mindfulness practices provides a powerful tool for nurturing mental well-being. It offers individuals a way to cultivate a deeper connection with themselves, manage stress, and foster a sense of calm amidst the demands of daily life.

Prioritizing self-care in a busy world

Prioritizing self-care in a busy world is crucial for maintaining overall well-being and managing stress effectively. In today's fast-paced society, it's easy to get caught up in the demands of work, family, and other responsibilities, often neglecting our own needs in the process. However, self-care is not a luxury but a necessity.

To prioritize self-care, it's important to recognize that taking care of yourself is not selfish, but rather a prerequisite for being able to fulfill your obligations and responsibilities to the best of your ability. Here are some steps you can take to prioritize self-care:

1. Assess your needs: Take a moment to reflect on your physical, emotional, and mental well-being. What activities or practices help you relax, rejuvenate, and recharge? Identify your personal self-care needs and preferences.

2. Set boundaries: Learn to say no when necessary and establish healthy boundaries. Overcommitting yourself can lead to burnout and prevent you from taking care of yourself. It's okay to prioritize your well-being and decline certain obligations or delegate tasks when possible.

3. Schedule self-care activities: Treat self-care as an essential appointment in your calendar. Dedicate specific time slots for activities that promote relaxation, such as exercise, meditation, hobbies, or spending time with loved ones. Protect this time and commit to it as you would any other commitment.

4. Practice mindfulness: Incorporate mindfulness into your daily routine. Take moments throughout the day to check in with yourself, observe your thoughts and emotions without judgment, and engage in deep breathing exercises. Mindfulness can help reduce stress and improve overall well-being.

5. Prioritize sleep and nutrition: Ensure you're getting enough sleep and maintaining a balanced diet. Adequate rest and nourishment are fundamental for physical and mental health. Prioritize quality sleep and make conscious choices about the foods you consume to support your well-being.

6. Delegate and seek support: Don't hesitate to ask for help or delegate tasks when possible. Surround yourself with a support system that understands the importance of self-care and can provide assistance when needed. Remember, you don't have to do everything on your own.

7. Disconnect from technology: Take regular breaks from screens and technology. Constant connectivity can be draining and overwhelming. Engage in activities that allow you to unplug and disconnect, such as spending time in nature, reading a book, or engaging in creative pursuits.

Remember that self-care is a continuous practice and may look different for everyone. It's about intentionally carving out time and space to nurture your physical, emotional, and mental well-being. By prioritizing self-care, you can cultivate a healthier and more balanced life in a busy world.

Exploring holistic approaches to mental health, including nutrition, exercise, and sleep
Exploring holistic approaches to mental health involves considering various factors beyond traditional therapeutic interventions. It emphasizes the interconnection between physical well-being and mental well-being, recognizing that nutrition, exercise, and sleep play significant roles in maintaining good mental health.

Nutrition is an essential aspect of mental health. A balanced diet that includes nutrient-rich foods can provide the necessary vitamins, minerals, and antioxidants that support brain function. Certain nutrients, such as omega-3 fatty acids found in fish and nuts, have been linked to improved mood and cognitive function. A poor diet lacking in essential nutrients can contribute to mental health issues.

Exercise has numerous benefits for mental health. Physical activity promotes the release of endorphins, which are natural mood enhancers. Regular exercise can reduce symptoms of anxiety and depression, improve self-esteem, and increase overall well-being. Engaging in activities like walking, running, yoga, or team sports can have positive effects on mental health by reducing stress and improving cognitive function.

Sleep plays a vital role in maintaining mental health and well-being. Sufficient and quality sleep is essential for optimal brain function, emotional regulation, and memory consolidation. Lack of sleep or poor sleep quality can lead to increased stress, irritability, difficulty concentrating, and impaired cognitive abilities. Establishing a consistent sleep routine, creating a conducive sleep environment, and practicing relaxation techniques can contribute to better sleep patterns and improved mental health.

By adopting a holistic approach to mental health that incorporates nutrition, exercise, and sleep, individuals can enhance their overall well-being. It is important to consult with healthcare professionals or experts in these respective fields to develop personalized strategies and interventions that cater to individual needs and circumstances.

Seeking Professional Help

Understanding the role of mental health professionals

Understanding the role of mental health professionals is crucial in promoting and supporting individuals' well-being and mental health. Mental health professionals encompass a wide range of practitioners, including psychiatrists, psychologists, counselors, social workers, and psychiatric nurses.

Psychiatrists are medical doctors specializing in mental health. They can diagnose mental health conditions, prescribe medication, and provide comprehensive treatment plans. Psychologists are trained in assessing and treating mental health disorders through therapy and psychological interventions. They often focus on psychotherapy to help individuals address emotional and behavioral challenges.

Counselors are professionals who provide guidance and support to individuals experiencing various mental health issues. They may specialize in specific areas such as marriage and family therapy, addiction counseling, or career counseling. Social workers play a crucial role in connecting individuals to essential resources, such as housing, financial assistance, and community support services. They also provide counseling and advocate for clients' rights.

Psychiatric nurses work in collaboration with psychiatrists to administer medication, monitor patients' progress, and provide supportive care. They play a vital role in both inpatient and outpatient settings, ensuring the holistic well-being of individuals.

Mental health professionals work with individuals of all ages and backgrounds, addressing a wide range of mental health concerns, including anxiety, depression, substance abuse, trauma, and more. They employ evidence-based practices and therapeutic techniques to help individuals manage symptoms, develop coping strategies, and improve their overall quality of life.

Moreover, mental health professionals play a crucial role in destigmatizing mental health issues and raising awareness about the importance of mental well-being. They may also engage in research, advocacy, and community education to promote mental health and contribute to advancements in the field.

Overall, mental health professionals are dedicated to helping individuals navigate their mental health challenges, providing support, guidance, and effective treatment to promote recovery and overall well-being.

20

Identifying when and how to seek therapy or counseling

1. Recognizing the Need: Consider seeking therapy or counseling if you're experiencing persistent emotional distress, struggling with relationships, facing major life transitions, or dealing with mental health concerns like anxiety or depression. Recognizing and acknowledging these challenges is the first step towards seeking help.

2. Assessing the Impact: Evaluate how these challenges are affecting your daily life, relationships, work, or overall well-being. If you notice significant disruptions or if your ability to function is impaired, it might be time to seek professional assistance.

3. Trust Your Instincts: Listen to your intuition. If you have a persistent feeling that something isn't right or that you would benefit from professional guidance, trust your gut. You know yourself best, and it's essential to prioritize your mental health.

4. Research and Find a Therapist: Look for qualified therapists or counselors who specialize in the areas you're struggling with. You can seek recommendations from trusted friends, family, or healthcare professionals. Online directories and professional associations can also provide valuable resources.

5. Initial Consultation: Many therapists offer initial consultations, which allow you to assess if you feel comfortable and connected with the therapist. Use this opportunity to discuss your concerns and treatment approach. Finding the right therapist-client fit is crucial for effective therapy.

6. Financial Considerations: Understand the financial aspects of therapy, including the cost per session, insurance coverage, and available options if you have limited financial resources. Some therapists offer sliding-scale fees or community mental health centers may provide affordable services.

7. Overcoming Barriers: Recognize and address any potential barriers that may hinder your access to therapy, such as transportation, childcare, or scheduling conflicts. Explore teletherapy options if in-person sessions are challenging to accommodate.

8. Confidentiality and Trust: Remember that therapy is a confidential space where you can share your thoughts, emotions, and concerns openly. Establishing trust and feeling safe with your therapist is crucial for productive therapy sessions.

9. Regularity and Commitment: Commit to attending therapy regularly and being actively engaged in the process. Therapy requires effort and dedication, and progress often takes time. Be patient with yourself and trust the therapeutic process.

10. Building a Support System: Therapy can be complemented by building a strong support network of family, friends, or support groups. These individuals can provide additional emotional support and understanding outside of therapy sessions.

Remember, seeking therapy or counseling is a personal decision, and it's essential to prioritize your mental well-being. A qualified mental health professional can provide tailored guidance and support as you navigate your challenges and work towards positive change.

Breaking down the various treatment modalities and interventions available
The different treatment modalities and interventions available in healthcare.

1. Medication: One common treatment modality involves the use of medications to manage various conditions and diseases. Medications can target specific symptoms, alleviate pain, or address underlying causes.

2. Psychotherapy: Also known as talk therapy, psychotherapy involves meeting with a mental health professional to discuss and address emotional or psychological challenges. It can help individuals gain insight, develop coping strategies, and improve their overall well-being.

3. Physical Therapy: This treatment modality focuses on improving physical function and mobility. Physical therapists use exercises, manual techniques, and other interventions to reduce pain, restore movement, and enhance strength and flexibility.

4. Surgery: In cases where other interventions are insufficient, surgery may be necessary. Surgical procedures involve the physical alteration or repair of tissues or organs to treat diseases, injuries, or abnormalities.

5. Alternative and Complementary Therapies: These treatment modalities encompass a wide range of approaches that complement traditional medicine. Examples include acupuncture, chiropractic care, herbal medicine, and meditation. While their effectiveness may vary, some individuals find them beneficial as part of their overall treatment plan.

6. Rehabilitation: Rehabilitation interventions are designed to help individuals recover, regain skills, and improve quality of life after an injury, illness, or surgery. This may involve physical, occupational, or speech therapy, depending on the specific needs of the individual.

7. Lifestyle Modifications: Making changes to one's lifestyle can be an effective treatment modality for certain conditions. This may include adopting a healthier diet, engaging in regular exercise, managing stress, improving sleep patterns, and avoiding harmful substances.

It's important to note that the choice of treatment modality and interventions depends on the specific condition, individual needs, and healthcare professional recommendations. A comprehensive approach often involves a combination of these modalities to achieve the best possible outcomes for the patient.

22

Breaking the Stigma

Challenging societal stigmas surrounding mental health
Addressing societal stigmas surrounding mental health is a complex and important task. It involves challenging deep-rooted beliefs, biases, and misconceptions that contribute to the discrimination and marginalization of individuals with mental health conditions. Here are some key aspects of tackling these stigmas:

1. Education and Awareness: Promote education and raise awareness about mental health to dispel myths and misconceptions. Encourage open discussions, provide accurate information, and share personal stories to humanize the experiences of those with mental health challenges.

2. Media Representation: Advocate for responsible and accurate portrayals of mental health in media. Encourage depictions that avoid sensationalism, stereotypes, and stigmatizing language, and instead promote empathy, understanding, and recovery.

3. Language Matters: Promote the use of person-centered language that emphasizes the individual over their condition. Avoid derogatory terms or labels that perpetuate negative stereotypes. Encourage respectful and compassionate communication when discussing mental health.

4. Empathy and Support: Foster a culture of empathy and support by encouraging individuals to listen, validate, and offer assistance to those struggling with mental health challenges. Promote the understanding that mental health is a shared human experience and that seeking help is a sign of strength, not weakness.

5. Policy and Legislation: Advocate for policies and legislation that protect the rights and well-being of individuals with mental health conditions. This includes ensuring access to affordable and quality mental health services, promoting anti-discrimination measures, and supporting workplace accommodations.

6. Collaboration and Partnerships: Work collaboratively with mental health organizations, community leaders, healthcare providers, and other stakeholders to collectively challenge stigmas and promote mental health awareness. Engage in campaigns, events, and initiatives that aim to normalize conversations around mental health.

7. Personal Reflection and Growth: Encourage individuals to examine their own biases and attitudes towards mental health. Foster a culture of personal growth and self-reflection to challenge any stigmatizing beliefs and promote understanding and acceptance.

By actively challenging societal stigmas surrounding mental health through these approaches, we can create a more inclusive and supportive environment for individuals with mental health conditions, promoting their well-being and overall societal health.

Promoting open dialogue and acceptance

Promoting open dialogue and acceptance creates an environment that encourages individuals to freely express their thoughts, opinions, and experiences without facing judgment or discrimination. It involves fostering respectful and inclusive conversations that embrace diverse perspectives and foster mutual understanding. Through open dialogue, people can engage in constructive discussions, exchange ideas, and gain insights from one another. This leads to greater empathy, tolerance, and acceptance of various beliefs, cultures, and identities. Ultimately, this approach cultivates inclusive communities and contributes to a more harmonious and compassionate society.

Advocating for mental health awareness and support systems

Advocating for mental health awareness involves promoting understanding, education, and destigmatization surrounding mental health issues. It emphasizes the importance of recognizing and addressing mental health concerns in society. By raising awareness, individuals and organizations can help reduce the stigma associated with mental health and encourage people to seek support when needed.

Support systems for mental health refer to the networks and resources available to individuals facing mental health challenges. These systems can include professional mental health services, such as therapy or counseling, as well as community-based programs, helplines, and online resources. The goal of support systems is to provide accessible, compassionate, and effective care to individuals struggling with mental health issues, helping them navigate their difficulties and improve their well-being.

Advocating for mental health awareness and support systems involves advocating for policies, funding, and resources to ensure that mental health is prioritized within communities, institutions, and healthcare systems. It also involves promoting open dialogue about mental health, encouraging individuals to share their experiences and seek help without fear of judgment or discrimination.

By advocating for mental health awareness and support systems, we can work towards creating a society that recognizes the significance of mental well-being, offers accessible resources, and supports individuals on their journey to recovery and overall mental wellness.

Supporting Others: Families, Communities, and Institutions

Nurturing mental health in family dynamics

Nurturing mental health within family dynamics involves creating a supportive and caring environment that promotes the well-being of each family member. Here are some key aspects to consider:

1. Open Communication: Encourage open and honest communication within the family. Create a safe space where family members can express their thoughts, feelings, and concerns without judgment. Active listening and empathetic responses are essential in fostering understanding and connection.

2. Emotional Support: Show unconditional love and support to family members. Offer empathy, validation, and reassurance during difficult times. Encourage sharing emotions and provide comfort when needed. This helps individuals feel understood and reduces feelings of isolation.

3. Healthy Boundaries: Establishing and respecting healthy boundaries is crucial. Encourage each family member to express their needs and preferences, while also understanding and respecting the boundaries of others. This fosters a sense of autonomy, promotes healthy relationships, and reduces conflicts.

4. Quality Time: Allocate dedicated time for shared activities and bonding. Engage in regular family rituals, such as family meals or outings, where everyone can come together, enjoy each other's company, and strengthen their connections. These moments help build positive experiences and memories.

5. Supportive Environment: Create a nurturing environment that promotes well-being. This includes maintaining a healthy lifestyle through balanced nutrition, regular exercise, and sufficient sleep. Encourage healthy habits and provide resources or support for managing stress effectively.

6. Problem-Solving Skills: Teach problem-solving and conflict resolution skills within the family. Help family members develop effective communication techniques, negotiation skills, and the ability to find mutually beneficial solutions. This empowers individuals to address challenges constructively and strengthens family relationships.

7. Seek Professional Help: If any family member is experiencing persistent mental health issues or emotional distress, encourage seeking professional help. Mental health professionals can provide guidance, therapy, and support tailored to specific needs, helping individuals and the family navigate challenges more effectively.

Remember, nurturing mental health is an ongoing process that requires continuous effort and understanding. By prioritizing mental well-being and fostering a supportive family environment, you can contribute to the overall happiness and resilience of your family members.

Creating supportive communities and workplaces

Creating supportive communities and workplaces involves fostering environments where individuals feel valued, respected, and empowered. It entails building connections, promoting inclusivity, and providing resources and structures that enhance well-being and productivity.

In supportive communities, people come together to provide emotional support, encouragement, and a sense of belonging. This can be achieved through various means such as organizing social activities, establishing mentorship programs, and facilitating open communication channels. By nurturing positive relationships and fostering a culture of mutual support, communities can promote personal growth, resilience, and overall satisfaction.

In the context of workplaces, creating a supportive environment is crucial for employee engagement, satisfaction, and productivity. Employers can cultivate supportive workplaces by prioritizing open communication, listening to employee feedback, and implementing policies that promote work-life balance, flexibility, and inclusivity. This may involve initiatives like employee assistance programs, wellness initiatives, and diversity and inclusion training.

Supportive workplaces also recognize and address the needs of their employees, offering opportunities for professional development and growth. By fostering a culture of trust, collaboration, and recognition, organizations can create an environment where employees feel supported and motivated to excel.

Overall, creating supportive communities and workplaces involves fostering a sense of connection, providing resources and structures that enhance well-being, and promoting a culture of inclusivity and support. By prioritizing these aspects, communities and workplaces can foster positive relationships, growth, and overall thriving.

Advocating for mental health resources in educational institutions and healthcare systems

Advocating for mental health resources in educational institutions and healthcare systems involves raising awareness and promoting the importance of prioritizing mental well-being within these settings. It entails advocating for increased access to mental health services, support systems, and resources for individuals of all ages.

In educational institutions, advocating for mental health resources means pushing for the integration of mental health education and awareness programs into the curriculum. It involves promoting initiatives that address stigma, provide early intervention, and foster a supportive environment for students. This can include initiatives such as mental health workshops, counseling services, and student support groups.

Within healthcare systems, advocating for mental health resources aims to ensure that mental health services receive adequate funding, staffing, and attention. It involves pushing for the integration of mental health screenings and assessments into routine healthcare practices, as well as improving access to mental health professionals and treatment options. This can include advocating for policies that promote parity between mental and physical health coverage, increasing mental health research and innovation, and reducing barriers to accessing mental health care.

Overall, advocating for mental health resources in educational institutions and healthcare systems is about recognizing the importance of mental well-being and working towards creating environments that support individuals in their mental health journeys. It involves engaging stakeholders, raising awareness, and pushing for systemic changes to prioritize mental health and ensure that appropriate resources are available to those who need them.

Effects of Positive and Negative Mental Health

Good mental health has a profound impact on individuals, communities, nations, and the world as a whole. Here are some of the effects:

1. Individual Level: Good mental health enhances overall well-being and quality of life for individuals. It promotes positive emotions, resilience, and the ability to cope with stress effectively. Individuals with good mental health often experience improved self-esteem, higher levels of productivity, and better relationships with others.

2. Community Level: When individuals in a community have good mental health, it contributes to the overall social fabric and cohesion. People with positive mental health are more likely to engage in healthy relationships, participate actively in community activities, and contribute positively to their surroundings. This leads to stronger social connections, reduced social isolation, and a sense of belonging within the community.

3. National Level: Good mental health has significant implications for a nation's development and prosperity. Individuals with good mental health are more likely to be productive members of the workforce, leading to increased economic output. Furthermore, positive mental health reduces healthcare costs by decreasing the burden of mental health disorders and related comorbidities. It also fosters social stability, reduces crime rates, and promotes civic engagement, ultimately contributing to a healthier and more prosperous nation.

4. Global Level: The collective impact of good mental health across nations can positively influence the world at large. A mentally healthy global population promotes peace, cooperation, and understanding among diverse cultures and nations. It enhances international collaboration in addressing global challenges, such as climate change, poverty, and public health crises. Additionally, promoting mental health as a global priority helps reduce disparities and inequalities, ensuring that everyone has equal access to mental health support and resources.

Good mental health has far-reaching effects, from individual well-being to community cohesion, national development, and global harmony. Prioritizing mental health at all levels is crucial for creating a healthier, happier, and more resilient society.

Negative mental health can have far-reaching effects on individuals, communities, nations, and the world as a whole. Here are some of the impacts it can have:

1. Individual Effects: Negative mental health can severely impact an individual's overall well-being. It can lead to increased stress, anxiety, depression, and a reduced quality of life. It may also hinder personal relationships, limit educational and professional opportunities, and result in self-destructive behaviors such as substance abuse or self-harm.

2. Community Effects: In communities, the effects of negative mental health can be seen in various ways. It can strain relationships within families, leading to conflicts and breakdowns. It can also contribute to social isolation, as individuals may withdraw from social activities and engagements. Additionally, it can increase the burden on healthcare systems and social services, diverting resources away from other areas of need.

3. National Effects: Negative mental health impacts on a national level can be significant. It can lead to a decrease in productivity and work performance, resulting in economic losses. Mental health issues may also contribute to an increase in healthcare costs and a higher demand for mental health services. Furthermore, the stigma surrounding mental health can hinder effective policy development and the allocation of adequate resources for mental health care.

4. Global Effects: Mental health issues extend beyond national borders and have global implications. They contribute to a decrease in overall human capital, affecting workforce productivity on a global scale. Moreover, negative mental health can exacerbate social inequalities and create social unrest, impacting political stability and peace. Addressing mental health on a global level requires collaborative efforts, research, and the sharing of best practices to reduce the burden on individuals and societies worldwide.

The effects of negative mental health are wide-ranging and can impact individuals, communities, nations, and the world at large. Recognizing the importance of mental health and investing in prevention, early intervention, and comprehensive treatment can lead to healthier individuals, stronger communities, and more prosperous societies.

The Place of Spirituality

Spirituality can play a significant role in dealing with mental health. While mental health is a complex issue that often requires professional help, many individuals find solace and support through spiritual practices. Here are a few ways spirituality can contribute to mental well-being:

1. Meaning and Purpose: Spirituality can provide individuals with a sense of meaning and purpose in life, which can be particularly helpful during challenging times. Believing in something larger than oneself and having a sense of connection to a higher power or universal energy can offer comfort and hope.

2. Coping Mechanisms: Spiritual practices such as prayer, meditation, mindfulness, and contemplation can be powerful tools for managing stress, anxiety, and depression. These practices can promote relaxation, inner peace, and a sense of grounding, allowing individuals to better cope with their mental health challenges.

3. Social Support: Many spiritual communities offer a sense of belonging and social support. Being part of a community that shares similar beliefs and values can provide a supportive network of individuals who understand and empathize with mental health struggles. This sense of community can reduce feelings of isolation and provide a supportive environment for healing.

4. Self-Reflection and Growth: Spirituality often encourages self-reflection, introspection, and personal growth. Engaging in practices that foster self-awareness and understanding can help individuals identify and address underlying issues contributing to their mental health concerns. It can also provide a framework for personal transformation and healing.

5. Resilience and Hope: Spirituality can instill resilience by nurturing faith, hope, and optimism. Believing in the possibility of change and drawing strength from spiritual beliefs can empower individuals to persevere during difficult times. Spiritual teachings often emphasize the importance of acceptance, forgiveness, and gratitude, which can contribute to a more positive mindset.

It's important to note that spirituality is not a substitute for professional mental health care. It can be a valuable complement to traditional therapeutic approaches and medication, but it's crucial to seek appropriate help from trained professionals when needed. Each individual's spiritual journey is unique, and finding a balance that works for them is key.

Conclusion

"Unveiling the Mind" concludes by emphasizing the importance of prioritizing mental health in our lives and society as a whole. It encourages readers to embrace self-compassion, seek help when needed, and actively contribute to the destigmatization of mental health challenges. By fostering a compassionate and informed approach, we can collectively create a world that nurtures and supports the well-being of every individual's mind.

www.ingramcontent.com/pod-product-compliance
Lightning Source LLC
Chambersburg PA
CBHW070235260726
48658CB00006BA/2340